BUT WHY ?

DO FISH BREATHE UNDER WATER?

AND OTHER SILLY QUESTIONS FROM CURIOUS KIDS

BUT WHY

DO FISH BREATHE UNDERWATER?
AND OTHER SILLY QUESTIONS FROM CURIOUS KIDS

by Jane Lindholm and Melody Bodette
illustrations by Neil Swaab

GROSSET & DUNLAP

GROSSET & DUNLAP
An imprint of Penguin Random House LLC, New York

First published in the United States of America by Grosset & Dunlap,
an imprint of Penguin Random House LLC, New York, 2022

Text copyright © 2022 by Jane Lindholm and Melody Bodette

Illustrations on the following pages copyright © 2022 by Neil Swaab:
cover, iii, iv, viii, 1, 3–4 (clouds), 5, 6, 11, 13, 18, 19, 27, 29, 35, 36, 39,
42 (bubbles), 43, 53, 56, 59 (seahorse, bubbles), 64, 67, 73, 74, 76, 81,
83, 95, 96, 110, 112–117 (shark teeth), 123, 125, 126–127, 130

Photo on page 30: Kimpin/Adobe Stock

Author photo on page vii by Jane Lindholm and Melody Bodette

Photos and illustrations not listed above are from Getty Images.

GROSSET & DUNLAP is a registered trademark of Penguin Random House LLC.

Visit us online at penguinrandomhouse.com.

Library of Congress Cataloging-in-Publication Data is available.

Manufactured in China

ISBN 9780593384367   10 9 8 7 6 5 4 3 2 1 TOPL

CONTENTS

~~~~~~~~~~~~~~~~~~~~~~

INTRODUCTION

DO YOU KNOW WHY OCEANS ARE SALTY? OR WHY IT'S easier to float in the ocean than in a pond? Do you know what jellyfish are made of? Or why seals bark, whales sing, and clams squirt? Don't worry if you don't know the answers yet, because you will soon!

But Why started out as a podcast for curious kids. The podcast is produced by Vermont Public Radio and is made by us, Melody Bodette and Jane Lindholm. We receive questions from kids all over the world, and it's our job to find answers. Now we're expanding to books! In this book we're answering questions from real kids like you, questions all about the ocean.

You'll learn lots of interesting, silly, and even bizarre facts about the ocean and the things that live in it. You might even learn about how you could help save the ocean from pollution (but only if you

BUT WHY

go to Chapter 11 to read more)!

But before we get too deep, let's dive in and answer some of the questions kids have been sending us about the ocean!

If you still have questions when you're done reading, send them our way, and we'll see if we can include them in a future podcast episode or book. Go to page 136 to learn more about how to send in your own questions.

And, as we always say: Stay curious!

CHAPTER 1
THE SALTY SEA AND THE WILD WAYS OF WAVES

THE OCEAN COVERS MORE THAN 70 PERCENT OF THE surface of our earth and is home to plants, animals, birds, and bacteria (and even sunken ships!). Humans rely on the ocean for transportation and recreation (having fun), for food, and for all kinds of products we use in our everyday lives. And the ocean has a lot to do with our weather and the temperature of the earth on land as well! Technically, there is only one global ocean—but you have probably heard of the Atlantic, Pacific, Indian, and Arctic oceans, and maybe the Southern (or Antarctic) ocean, too. So, what gives?

Well, an **ocean** is one large, interconnected body of salt water where water can flow freely from one area to another. Most of the salt water on earth, what we think of as ocean water, is all connected. So, we really have one ocean. We're not suggesting you try, but if you wanted to, you *could* sail all around the world without ever having to set foot on land!

It would get pretty confusing if all that water all around the world was just labeled OCEAN on our maps. The different parts of the global ocean have instead been named—and fought over—just like the world's lands have been. There are also other parts of the ocean that have different names. The National Geographic Society says there are about fifty **seas** around the world— these are usually parts of the ocean that are partially bordered by land. Then there are bays, gulfs, **isthmuses** (say: isth-mis), and straits, all just different parts of the global ocean. (Go to page 51 for more definitions of all the different terms we use to describe bodies of water.)

Within all that water, there are a lot of really different kinds of places. In some spots the ocean surface water is eighty or ninety degrees Fahrenheit—nearly as warm as a bathtub! Colder ocean areas might have surface water that is actually below the temperature at which water freezes—giving them a top layer of sea ice. Brrrr!

The seafloor is as geographically diverse as dry land, too. There are deep trenches and tall mountains— some poking above the surface as islands. And the depth of the ocean varies widely from place to place. The average depth of the ocean is a little under two miles. But in one spot in the western Pacific Ocean

known as the Challenger Deep, it's nearly seven miles down to the bottom! That means you could fit Mount Everest in that trench and still have more than a mile of ocean above the peak. (You can read more about Challenger Deep in Chapter 4.)

There are even parts of the seafloor where no light penetrates; some of the animals that live down there have no eyes. There are other areas filled with all sorts of sea life, like fish, sharks, jellyfish,  whales, and even narwhals. (Yes, narwhals are real!)

Humans have always been fascinated by the ocean. But there are still areas we don't know much about because they are so difficult to explore. Later on in the book, you'll learn about an international project that aims to map the entire ocean floor by 2030. But even once we have a map, there's still so much more to discover. Maybe one day when you grow up, you'll explore these fascinating areas of earth!

WHY IS THE SEA SALTY?

—BEN, 4, NORTH CAROLINA

GREAT QUESTION, BEN! HAVE YOU EVER LICKED YOUR LIPS
after going for a swim in the ocean? If you have,
you probably noticed a distinctly salty flavor. To
understand why the ocean is salty, you actually have to
start with rainwater. Rain is slightly **acidic**, meaning
that over long periods of time the water can erode the
rocks it lands on when it falls to earth. To **erode** means
to naturally wear away. Some of the minerals from the
rocks are washed away by the rain. Salt is one of those
minerals.

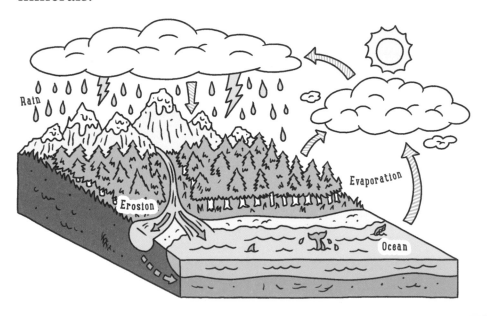

The salt washes into streams, and streams run into rivers, and eventually all that water runs to the ocean, carrying the salt and other minerals it has picked up along the way. When that water gets to the ocean, there's nowhere else for it to go—rivers flow *to* the ocean, not *from* the ocean. So, the salt from all those different rivers just stays in the ocean, making the water salty.

On average, ocean water is about 3.5 percent salt by weight. This means that for every 100 pounds of water there is 3.5 pounds of salt. Because of climate change and pollution, some of the world's water may actually be getting a little bit saltier these days.

There are also a few lakes that are salty! These are lakes with no **outlets**—that is, no rivers for the water to flow out of the lake. So, the lakes collect salt and minerals just like the ocean. The Great Salt Lake in Utah, and the Dead Sea, between the countries of Jordan and Israel, are both much saltier than the ocean!

SALTY!

WHY IS IT EASIER TO FLOAT IN SALT WATER?

You might not be able to *see* the difference between salt water and fresh water just by looking at it, but you may *feel* the difference when you go for a swim! Why? The short answer is density, the measure of an object's mass per volume.

The long answer is this: Salt water is more dense than fresh water. Now, this might sound a little confusing (so bear with us!), but the same amount (volume) of salt water has more mass than fresh water, which in a way, makes it heavier. So, when you go for a swim in the ocean, your body floats better in the dense salt water than it would in your tub or a freshwater lake because your body is less dense (less heavy) than the salt water!

Remember the Dead Sea? Well, the salt concentration in the Dead Sea is almost ten times the amount of salt in the ocean, so you can practically float like a cork in that water! You can try this for yourself by filling two bowls with fresh water. Add some salt to one of the bowls and stir to help it dissolve. Then grab something in your house that floats, like a Ping-Pong ball or a bath toy, and put it in one bowl and then the other. See if you can tell the difference just by looking!

HOW IS CLIMATE CHANGE AFFECTING THE OCEAN?

—OWEN, 6, SOUTH CAROLINA

TO UNDERSTAND CLIMATE CHANGE, OWEN, YOU FIRST HAVE to understand climate. Climate is connected to weather, but they're not exactly the same. **Weather** is what's happening in the atmosphere on any given day—rain or snow, clear or cloudy, hot or cold. **Climate** is the trend of the weather over time. Here's an easy way to remember the difference: picture a dog on a leash being walked by its owner down a sidewalk. The dog may wander from one side of the sidewalk to the other (this is weather), but the general direction, or trend, of the dog is straight ahead (this is climate).

Over the last hundred years, scientists say the average temperature on earth has risen by two degrees Fahrenheit. That may not seem like much. After all, a change of a few degrees on any given day is barely noticeable. But over time, a rise in the overall temperature on earth could lead to some big changes, like rising sea levels and unpredictable weather patterns.

The earth has had a lot of changes in its long history. (Check out page 91 to learn about a time when much of the northern half of the earth was completely covered by snow and ice!) Change in the earth's climate and landscape over time is a natural part of the earth's evolution. But most scientists agree that the increase in temperature the earth is experiencing now is very fast and caused primarily by human activity.

Humans use a lot of what are called **fossil fuels**—oil and gas used to power factories, cars, planes, and even our homes. When we burn those fuels, we're releasing carbon dioxide into the atmosphere. When the sun's rays come through the atmosphere, they heat the surface of the earth. That heat should bounce off the earth, back into space. But when there's a lot of carbon dioxide in the atmosphere, it tends to hold too much of that heat, making the surface of the earth and the ocean warmer. The last twenty years have included some of the warmest years of the century.

So, what's the problem? Well, this added warmth is causing polar regions, where there are lots of icebergs and other kinds of ice, to warm up. Melting ice causes more water to run into the sea, which makes the sea level rise; this could threaten cities built near the water. And many of the plants and animals in the ocean need a certain climate and ecosystem to survive. This drastic change in climate could lead to **extinction** (dying off) for many species.

More carbon dioxide in the atmosphere also contributes to a process that makes the ocean more acidic, as the water in the ocean tries to absorb more carbon dioxide out of the atmosphere. That makes it more difficult for ocean species that have a hard shell, like shellfish and coral, to get enough calcium and carbonate out of the water to make those shells. Softer shells make them more susceptible to predators.

To learn more about what you can do to help reduce the negative effects of climate change, see Chapter 11.

WHY ARE THERE WAVES IN THE SEA?
—SAMUEL, 7, UNITED KINGDOM

THERE ARE DIFFERENT KINDS OF WAVES—NOT JUST THE WET kind—but they all have something in common: Waves move energy through space. In the ocean, waves move energy through water. The water itself isn't moving much. When you see a wave, it is actually energy moving through the water and creating the shape of a wave as it passes from one place to another.

The most common type of wave in the ocean is a surface wave, which is caused by wind moving across the top of the water. The friction between the wind and the water creates a wave. **Friction** is how difficult it is for two objects to keep moving as they rub against one another. The force of the wind trying to blow across the top of the water causes the water to rise up as the wind goes by.

Big storms with strong winds can often cause larger than normal waves.

The moon's gravitational pull causes high and low tides.

The size of a wave that crashes onto shore can also be affected by the shape of the land underneath it. An area with a long, shallow beach and a sheltered bay will likely have pretty calm water. A beach where the wind blows a great distance and the ground underneath the waves drops off steeply will likely have larger and stronger shoreline waves.

Waves can also be caused by disturbances underneath the water, like a volcano or an earthquake. Those types of waves are often called **tsunamis** (say: soo-NAH-mes), and are sometimes very dangerous because they roll up on shore much farther inland than typical waves do. The largest tsunami ever recorded, in the Gulf of Alaska, created a wall of water 1,720 feet high. That's higher than the Empire State Building in New York! But don't worry—tsunamis are quite rare.

The sun and the moon also play a role in the waves, by creating tides. A **tide** is actually one big wave with smaller surface waves on top of it.

You probably know that the earth revolves around the sun. That's because the sun has a force—called **gravity**—that pulls the earth toward it. (Because the earth is moving, it doesn't get sucked right into the sun, but instead rotates around it, making one full rotation each year.) The earth's gravity does the same thing for the moon. But the moon itself also has a **gravitational pull**—just big enough to move the water in the ocean a little bit toward it!

The ocean water closest to the moon is drawn closer by the tug of the moon's gravity, causing a sort of bulge that draws the water higher up the shoreline. That's known as high tide.

Because the water is being drawn closer to the moon on one side, the shoreline on the other side is lower down the shore. That's known as low tide. All shores experience two high tides and two low tides in the course of a full day.

Because the moon is much closer to the Earth than the sun is, the moon's gravitational pull has more of an effect on the ocean's tides. So, Samuel, the short answer to your question is that the sun, the moon, the seafloor, and the wind all contribute to those waves you see in the ocean!

WHERE DOES ALL THE SAND AT THE BEACH COME FROM?

—KIAN, 6, CALIFORNIA

ALL THAT SAND THAT'S SO MUCH FUN TO MAKE CASTLES out of and bury your toes in, Kian, is basically just teeny tiny pieces of rocks, or sometimes coral and seashells! Remember how we learned that the ocean is salty because of the minerals carried along by rivers and streams to the sea? Well, those rivers are also carrying little rocks that get smashed and bashed around as they travel downstream. Once they reach the ocean, they get crushed up even more by the waves, eventually getting small enough to be considered beach sand.

Some beaches have very fine sand and others have rough coarse sand. You can tell the difference pretty easily when you walk barefoot on a nice smooth beach versus one with lots of big rock and shell pieces. Ouch!

Not all beach sand is alike. Most of the world's beach sand is made up primarily of a rock called quartz. But you'll find black sand beaches in places like Hawaii that are made mostly of volcanic material, and white beaches in the Maldives that are the broken-down fragments of coral, seashells, and other organisms. Some of that sand is made by parrotfish, who eat the coral (more about coral next) and then poop it out—so the beach is actually made of parrotfish poop! Depending on the minerals and rocks it comes from, beach sand can be red, green, black, white, or tan. Look closely at the sand under your feet because it can tell you a lot about the landscape around you.

HELLOOOO!

HOW DO CORAL CHANGE COLORS?

—TEMPERANCE, 5, MICHIGAN

CORAL ARE BEAUTIFUL UNDERWATER SCULPTURES, AND, as Temperance has noticed, they can be red, green, brown, blue, mauve, or even purple. But what are they? Are they plants or animals or rocks? The answer is: yes!

Okay, let us explain . . .

Coral are actually **polyps**—little animals related to sea **anemones** (say: uh-NEM-uh-nees) and jellyfish. Polyps look like little cylinders with mouths at the top. Those mouths are surrounded by small arms—**tentacles**! Polyps pull the minerals calcium and carbonate out of the water to make a hard skeleton around their bodies for protection. When coral polyps die, they leave their skeletons behind, and more coral will be built on top of them, creating a rock. These coral skeletons will eventually make a big structure known as a coral reef. A famous one is the Great Barrier Reef, off the coast of Australia, which is 1,400 miles long!

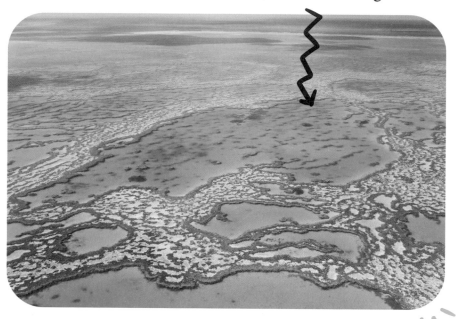

HOW DO CORAL EAT?
—LEILA, 6, MASSACHUSETTS

CORAL HAVE A SYMBIOTIC RELATIONSHIP WITH ALGAE (say: AL-jee), a plantlike organism, called **zooxanthellae** (say: zoh-uh-zan-THEL-ee). A **symbiotic relationship**

is when two species depend on each other. Those algae (zooxanthellae) live in the tissue of the coral polyps. The body of the polyp is clear and the algae in its tissue produces the colorful protein pigments that we see in coral. Coral live in shallow water with lots of sunlight. The zooxanthellae use that sunlight to produce their own food through photosynthesis. The algae also use the waste from the coral to feed on. In turn, coral polyps use some of the energy that the algae produce.

Coral reefs are the most biodiverse ecosystem in the ocean, according to the Coral Reef Alliance. They are home to thousands of species of fish as well as clams, shrimp, starfish, and sea turtles. Millions of humans depend on those species for their survival. Yet, coral are vulnerable to changes in ocean temperature, pollution, and human activity.

When water temperatures increase, coral basically kick out those zooxanthellae and turn white. This process is called **coral bleaching**. If coral stays white for too long and without those symbiotic algae to help them survive, the coral polyps will be placed in grave danger.

In 2012, the World Resources Institute looked at the health of coral reefs around the world and determined that 75 percent of them are under threat. By 2050, *all* coral reefs in the world could be threatened if we don't take action. Scientists and researchers have been working hard to find ways to protect and preserve coral reefs. Maybe you'll be one of the people who helps reverse the trend!

WHAT IS OCEAN POLLUTION?

Ocean pollution is a *big* problem. Most of the pollution affecting the world's water comes from human activity on land in the form of chemicals and trash. Chemicals we use on things like lawns, farm fields, and roads run off the land into streams and waterways and eventually make their way to the ocean. Sometimes chemicals from our waste stream get into waterways, too—including medication that doesn't get broken down fully by our bodies. All these chemicals can cause problems for the animals and plants that live in the ocean, making their habitats unlivable for them, or causing changes in their bodies from ingesting (eating and drinking) man-made chemicals.

Noise pollution is also an issue. Too much noise from human activity like oil drilling, military sonar, and even just boat noise, can make it difficult for animals like whales to communicate over long distances.

Plastic trash is another concern. There is a huge floating mass of plastic and trash swirling around in the Pacific Ocean that is spread out over more than six hundred thousand square miles. This mass is known as the Great Pacific Garbage Patch. It's more than three times the size of Spain and more than six times the size of the United Kingdom.

CLEAN OUR OCEAN!

Alli Maloney, a writer for *Teen Vogue*, took a trip to see what this looks like. "In the water itself," she told us, "you can see broken pieces of plastic. We could see everything from buckets to traffic cones . . . I remember seeing what looked like the front of an air conditioning unit just kind of floating by in the water." She said there are also a lot of fishing lines and other trash left behind by fishing boats.

But it's not just big garbage on the surface of the water. "Underneath the water surface," Maloney said, "there's all of these teeny tiny pieces, these fragments of plastic. So those bigger pieces I saw floating, they break down further and further and further, but they never fully go away. And the bottom of the ocean, especially in the Great Pacific Garbage Patch, is full of it."

All of this trash causes lots of problems for ocean wildlife. Not only is it a nuisance, but sometimes animals eat the trash or get stuck in it and can die. Sometimes heavy metal chemicals that leach out of the plastic trash get into the water and harm animals. International laws are in place to help reduce marine pollution, but we all need to do our part to use less plastic and fewer unnecessary chemicals to help protect the ocean (more on this in Chapter 11).

CHAPTER 2
SHELLFISH: HERMIT CRABS, OYSTERS, AND CLAMS THAT SQUIRT

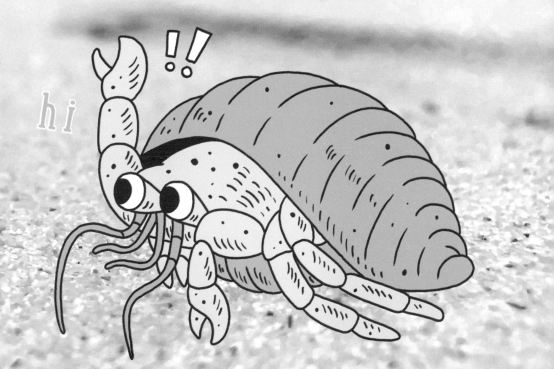

HOW DO SEASHELLS GET INTO THE OCEAN? —ALICE, 6, LOUISIANA

IF YOU WALK ON A BEACH EARLY IN THE MORNING, ALICE,
you might be lucky enough to find a beautiful seashell
washed up on shore, or perhaps a sand
dollar or snail shell. Have you
ever wondered how all these
shells ended up here?

All of those shells
were once homes for
mollusks. Mollusks are
invertebrates (say: in-VER-
tuh-bretts), meaning they have
no backbones. Many mollusks have
external shells, known as exoskeletons. Some have just
one shell, like limpets or snails. Others have two shells
that join with a hinge, like oysters, clams, mussels, and
scallops. Shells protect the soft bodies of the mollusks.
(Interestingly, squid, cuttlefish, and octopuses are also
mollusks, even though they don't have external shells.
They have other ways of defending themselves, which
you can read about on page 75.)

Mollusks come out of their eggs without hard shells. But within days they begin building a sturdy home around themselves. They use a part of their body called the mantle to build their shell out of calcium carbonate from the water and proteins from their own bodies. They live in the shell for the rest of their lives. They can increase the size of the shell as they grow, and they can even repair cracks or breaks in it!

When they die, their soft bodies decompose (naturally break down), but those shells are still useful to other creatures! Hermit crabs move into abandoned sea snail shells (and then swap for a bigger one when they need more room). Small fish use empty shells to hide from predators. Birds sometimes use shells in nests. And as we learned earlier, some shells even become the sand you walk on. So if you find a pretty shell on the seashore, it's probably best to leave it on the beach!

WHY DO CLAMS SQUIRT?

—LYLA, 4, WASHINGTON

CLAMS HAVE AN ORGAN CALLED A SIPHON (SAY: SIGH-FIN), a long part of their body that can poke out of the shell. It's sometimes called the clam's neck. Clams bury themselves deep in the sand to stay wet and to hide from predators, with their siphon sticking straight up out of the shell. This lets clams take in water that they need in order to breathe and filter feed, and it also allows them to squirt water out! When a predator approaches, they sometimes dig down deeper, pushing water up as they go. So if you see a little jet of water spraying out from the sand, there's probably a clam down below.

SQUIRT
SQUIRT
SQUIRT

HOW DO OYSTERS MAKE PEARLS?

—SIGGA, 8, OREGON

A PEARL IS THE BEAUTIFUL RESULT OF THE ANIMAL TRYING to stop something from irritating it, like a bit of sand or a parasite in the oyster's soft body. The oyster will begin to produce a substance called **nacre** (say: NAY-kur), also known as mother-of-pearl, the same shiny substance that lines the inside of the oyster shell. The oyster covers the irritating bit with layers of nacre—and that's what the pearl is! Ocean oysters and freshwater mussels both make pearls.

Pearls are created naturally, but because humans think they're pretty and use them for jewelry, we've also figured out how to get oysters to make them more frequently than they would naturally. Essentially, it's pearl farming. In fact, most of the pearls you see are cultured, which means they were intentionally made, rather than grown naturally on their own.

PRETTY!

WHY DO WE HEAR THE OCEAN IN SHELLS?—SAWYER, 6, VERMONT

WHEN YOU PUT A BIG SHELL UP TO your ear, you know the ocean isn't really inside it. So why does it sometimes sound like you can hear the crashing of waves? Well, Sawyer, it's not magic, just a little wishful thinking.

When people put a big seashell up to their ear at the beach, they're probably hearing the wind and waves all around them, filtered through the hard and echoey chamber of a shell. Even if you're not at the beach, when you hold a shell tightly to your ear, you are hearing whatever background noise is around you— wind, people talking, fans—but it sounds different because the shell is amplifying (turning up) the sound in a different way as it travels through the shell to your ear. Because shells come from the beach, it's easy to think that's the sound of the ocean you're hearing!

Test this out by holding a jar or a glass to your ear at home. What does it sound like to you?

WHAT ARE STARFISH?

Starfish aren't fish at all. They and their cousins—sea urchins, sea cucumbers, and sea lilies—are all echinoderms (say: ee-KYE-nuh-derms), a group of animals whose name means "spiny skin."

Starfish are more aptly called sea stars. They have a central body and radiating arms. Most people picture a sea star with five arms, but some have as many as twenty or forty! They are carnivores that eat mollusks and barnacles. (A barnacle is a small crustacean (say: crust-AY-shin), in the same family as shrimp, crabs, and lobsters. They "glue" themselves to rocks with a natural cement that's incredibly sticky.)

Sea stars can live up to thirty-five years. And if a predator tries to bite one of their arms, they can release it from their body and grow a new one. In fact, some sea stars can grow a whole new body just from a severed arm itself. We don't know whether you'll think this is cool or gross, but when they eat, the stomach of the sea star pokes out through its mouth and surrounds its prey, sucking it up and digesting it before going back inside the sea star's body.

Want to know about those other echinoderms? Sea urchins are often round with a central mouth for eating small prey. Sand dollars are burrowing sea urchins, and that "dollar" you might find is their hard outer body. Sand dollars washed up on the beach are usually dried out, but when they're alive, sand dollars are just as spiky as other sea urchins.

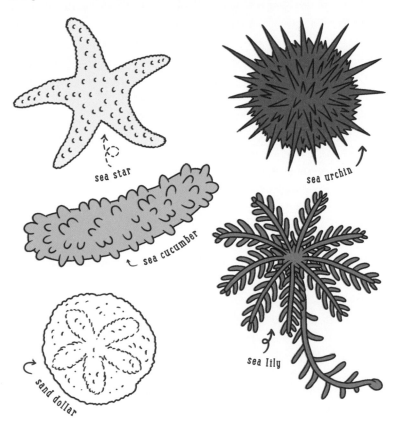

sea star

sea urchin

sea cucumber

sand dollar

sea lily

While you might find sea urchins and sea stars in a shallow tide pool near the water's edge, sea cucumbers live deep in the ocean. And they really do look like an underwater cucumber!

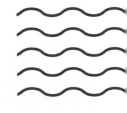

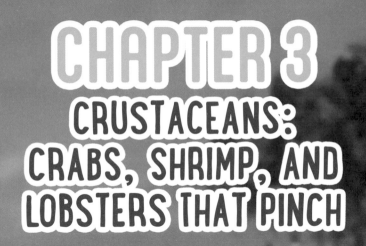

CHAPTER 3
CRUSTACEANS:
CRABS, SHRIMP, AND
LOBSTERS THAT PINCH

NOW WE'RE GOING TO LEARN ABOUT A GROUP OF ANIMALS called **crustaceans**. If you've ever seen a crab or shrimp, a lobster, or a crayfish, you've seen a crustacean! Crustaceans are arthropods. **Arthropods** wear their skeletons on the outside. They include arachnids (spiders) and insects (like bees, ants, and beetles).

Like other arthropods, crustaceans don't have a backbone. Instead they have a hard exoskeleton—a shell, jointed legs, and segmented bodies. Crustaceans live in both fresh and salt water. Here's another cool feature: The eyes of crustaceans are usually on **stalks** (stick-like things) that stick up above their faces. Many also have antennae. Now, let's get to your questions about these cool creatures!

STICK EYES!

WHY DO LOBSTERS PINCH?

—ROMAN, 4, CALIFORNIA

WE HOPE YOU'RE NOT ASKING BECAUSE YOU'VE BEEN PINCHED by one, Roman! Those claws pack a serious pinch! That's why lobstermen and lobsterwomen slip rubber bands onto lobsters' claws after they're caught. It keeps the lobsters from fighting one another in the holding tank, and also prevents humans from getting pinched when they reach their hands in to grab them.

PINCH
PINCH
PINCH

Lobsters pinch to defend themselves, and to grab and tear their food. In a sheltered little beach called Kettle Cove, on the coast of southern Maine, we visited marine researcher Zach Whitener to learn more. The first thing Whitener did was peer into the cove's **tide pools**—rocky pools and puddles that stay full of water even at low tide. He was looking for a baby lobster so he could show us its claws. "When lobsters get under rocks, they'll excavate more to make a bigger home for themselves," he said as he struggled to lift a big barnacle-and-seaweed-covered rock. "So you can see where somebody has been digging under this rock."

As he finally moved the big rock we were looking at, Whitener spotted something moving. "Anybody home? Oh, there's one. Here's a baby, a juvenile lobster." The little lobster fit in the palm of Whitener's hands, but it was already a couple of years old. As we looked closer, we noticed this lobster was missing some things. It had no antennae, no eyes, and no claws! Whitener said this lobster's claws had probably been ripped off in a fight, possibly with another lobster.

If you look closely at most lobsters, you'll notice the two claws on a lobster look significantly different from each other. The bigger one is called the crusher claw.

PINCH
PINCH
PINCH

It's used to crush the shells of clams, crabs, and mussels that lobsters eat. The other is called the ripper claw, and it's used to tear softer food like fish. Lobsters have a dominant hand, just like most humans! If you look at a lobster, whichever side the crusher claw is on is that lobster's dominant side.

Here's something neat about lobsters Whitener told us while holding this wounded crustacean: "Lobsters can regrow their limbs. So eventually his claws will grow back, and his antennae." Their legs will grow back, too, if they get one caught under a rock or if a predator grabs on to it. Whitener was unsure about what would happen with this one's eyes. But it seemed to be doing just fine without them. The injuries weren't new, and it didn't appear weak or sick, so Whitener lowered the rock and put the lobster back underneath it, where it could be safe to grow big and strong—and get its claws and antennae back!

OUCH!

WHY DO CRABS BLOW BUBBLES?

—HUGO, 4, VERMONT

IF YOU LOOK CLOSELY AT A CRAB, AS HUGO PROBABLY DID, you might see it blowing foamy bubbles out of its mouth! Crabs have gills, so they need water to be able to breathe, just like fish—they can't breathe air. However, these crustaceans have a unique adaptation that allows them to store water in their body to be used for breathing when they're on land (or being picked up in your hand). Some species can survive up to twelve hours out of the water, and others live most of their lives on land, returning to the water as adults to lay eggs. When you see a crab blowing bubbles, it's using the water in its body to breathe!

WHY DO CRABS WALK SIDEWAYS?

—ADELE, 3, AUSTRALIA

INTERESTINGLY, CRABS ACTUALLY *CAN* SHUFFLE FORWARD, but most crabs move sideways when they're on a mission. Crabs generally have ten limbs: this includes eight legs that they use for walking (four on each side of their body) and two front claws that they use for grabbing things. Their legs are hinged—like your knees!

Because of the way their joints bend out, moving side to side is their best way to get around. We probably think it's strange because we're so used to the way human legs are designed—but it's perfectly normal to a crab! Try it! Put your knees out to your sides. Now try to step forward. You'll find out pretty quickly that it's easier to go sideways.

It's worth noting that there are a few crab species that do walk in a forward motion, such as the soldier crab.

WHAT DO SHRIMP EAT?
—SAM, 5, BRITISH COLUMBIA

SAM, IT'S FUN TO THINK OF SHRIMP (AND CRABS, TOO) AS sort of the "ocean cleanup crew." Most crustaceans are **omnivores**, meaning they eat both plants and animals. These scavengers eat most anything they can find: dead

fish, worms, snails, algae, and plankton. Hey, this ocean floor isn't going to clean itself—time to call in the shrimp!

Shrimp can be as long as twelve inches or so small you can't really see them with the naked eye.

It's not just what shrimp and crabs eat that make them an important part of the ocean ecosystem— they're also

THAT'S ONE BIG SHRIMP!

a meal for many bigger ocean animals such as fish, sea stars, birds, dolphins, and sharks, and even other crabs and shrimp. They're also an important food for humans—maybe even you, Sam! Shrimp are the most commonly eaten seafood in the United States, according to the advocacy group Oceana. While shrimp live wild in the world's oceans, humans also farm them—on shrimp farms!

WHAT ARE PLANKTON?

These microscopic organisms can be either plantlike, known as phytoplankton (say: FIGHT-oh-plank-ton), or animals, known as zooplankton (say: ZOO-oh-plankton).

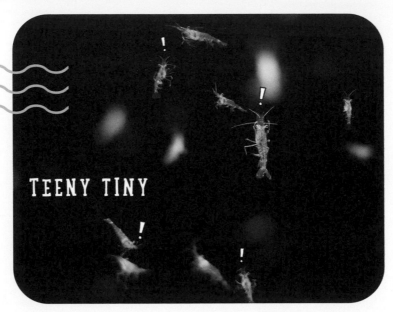

TEENY TINY

Phytoplankton are technically microscopic algae. They rely on the sun and the water to grow. And, like plants, phytoplankton give off oxygen. According to the National Oceanic and Atmospheric Association (NOAA), half of the oxygen on earth comes from the ocean, and much of that oxygen is made by phytoplankton.

Zooplankton include krill (which look like very small shrimp), sea snails, and even some types of marine worms. Some whales gulp down as many as 40 million krill per day!

Plankton means "drifter" in Greek. While a few types can swim, they're mostly pushed along by ocean currents. Each night zooplankton drift up from the bottom of the ocean to feed on the phytoplankton that have spent the day getting nutrients from the sun. This is the greatest migration on Earth, and NOAA says this movement can even be seen from space!

Plankton are crucial to a healthy ocean ecosystem. But threats like climate change are throwing ecosystems out of whack. In some parts of the ocean, plankton numbers are declining. In other places, phytoplankton can grow out of control, becoming the cause of toxic algae blooms like one known as red tide. The health of the world's plankton is important to the health of the entire planet.

RED TIDE!

CHAPTER 4
THE OCEAN'S GEOGRAPHY AND THE MYSTERY OF CHALLENGER DEEP

ONE OF THE NICKNAMES FOR EARTH IS THE blue planet. That's because when you look at Earth from space (we're told—we've never had the chance to go to space ourselves), it looks mostly blue. And *that's* because the earth is mostly water. More than two thirds of the globe is covered by water, and nearly all of the earth's water is in the ocean. The seafloor is as geographically diverse as dry land. So let's go a little deeper—into ocean geography!

We already mentioned that although there's really one big global ocean, it's divided up into five different parts: the Atlantic, the Pacific, the Arctic, the Indian, and the Southern (Antarctic) ocean basins.

In the same way that continents are divided up into countries, and countries are divided up into smaller regions like states, the ocean also gets divided up and named. It's a lot easier to identify what parts of the world we're talking about when they have different names.

The National Geographic Society says there are about fifty seas around the world—these are parts of the ocean that are usually partially bordered by land. Sometimes the word *sea* and the word *ocean* are used interchangeably. Like when we talk about seawater—that's the same thing as ocean water!

You can further break things down into **bays** (an area of water that is mostly separated from the main body of water by land that curves around it), **gulfs** (big bays), **coves** (small bays), **straits** (a narrow strip or passageway of water between two bigger bodies of water), and more—and that's just what you can see from the surface!

Underneath all that water, the ocean floor has all the same features you can see on land—there are plains, valleys, canyons, and even mountains! Some of these mountains poke above the water's surface as islands. All of the islands of Hawaii, for example, were formed by ocean volcanoes.

CHALLENGER DEEP

Just as humans have always explored the surface of the earth and are now keen on learning more about outer space, we've always been curious about the ocean, too. As technology has improved, we've been able to learn things about the ocean floor that we never knew before. For instance, we now know the average depth of the ocean is almost two miles. But! There is one area in the western Pacific Ocean where it's nearly seven miles down to the bottom! This area is known as Challenger Deep. You could fit six Grand Canyons in that trench!

Challenger Deep is the deepest known place on earth. It's so far down and under so much water that it is pitch-black and very cold. For a long time, scientists thought no life could survive down there.

This deep depression is part of a larger area known as the **Mariana Trench**. It was first discovered in 1875 by a British expedition that was trying to learn more about the ocean. The crew on the ship, known as the HMS *Challenger*, used sound devices and long weighted ropes to try to figure out how far down the seafloor was. Challenger Deep is named for that expedition that first alerted the world to just how deep the ocean might be.

Nearly a hundred years later, in 1960, for the first time two humans descended in a special diving vehicle all the way to the bottom. They discovered there were animals living even in the frigid inky darkness at the bottom of this trench.

As of 2021, very few people have ever gone all the way down to the bottom of Challenger Deep, though remote-controlled submersible vehicles have done other explorations of the area.

In fact, there's still a lot to explore on the ocean floor. Until just a few years ago, less than 10 percent of the seabed had been mapped. There is a lot of work being done right now to change that. A project known as Seabed 2030 is underway to have the whole ocean floor mapped by 2030, and then make that information available to the whole world.

The Seabed 2030 project uses teams all over the world to work on this mapping project. Vicki Ferrini, a senior research scientist at Columbia University, leads one of the regional centers. She says knowing more about what the bottom of the ocean looks like is really important!

"The shape of the ocean floor affects all sorts of different things," Ferrini told us. "It affects the way water circulates in the ocean, which can have an effect on climate. It can affect storms moving around— hurricanes are affected by water temperature."

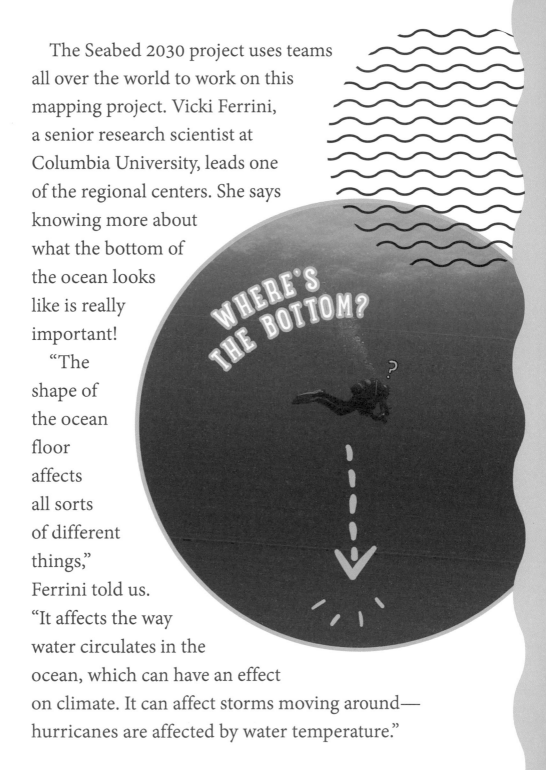

WHERE'S THE BOTTOM?

Water temperature can vary depending on the depth of the ocean, among other factors. Humans are dependent on fish and other resources on the seafloor for food and for metals we use to make things—so knowing more about the bottom of the ocean will help us understand the resources that are down there.

Even our technology is dependent on the surface of the seabed, Ferrini pointed out. "Actually, the communication we're using to talk on our phones, it doesn't go through the sky, it goes on cables on the seafloor. We don't even realize that every day all of us are very connected through the seafloor, which is pretty cool."

It's going to take a huge effort and a lot of money to map the entire seafloor by 2030. The project estimate is $3 billion to $5 billion! But having a map is just the beginning. Maybe *you* will be one of the scientists and explorers who helps us uncover the many mysteries that remain—not just about what the bottom of the ocean looks like, but what other animals, plants, and other mysteries can be found in this largest part of the planet on which we live.

CHAPTER 5
ARE SEAHORSES . . . HORSES? AND OTHER QUESTIONS ABOUT FISH

FISH ARE AQUATIC CREATURES WITH SKELETONS, SCALY skin, and fins that help them swim around in fresh or salt water. Most fish are adapted to live in either salt water or fresh water, but a few can live in both. These fish are called **anadromous** (say: uh-NAD-ruh-muss). Fish breathe through gills. **Gills** are a lot like lungs except the fish are breathing water instead of air! The gills take oxygen out of the water and expel carbon dioxide, just as our lungs do with air.

There is a huge variety of fish in the world's ocean waters—from fish that could fit on your fingernail to the giant whale shark, which can be bigger than a school bus! And fish come in all kinds of shapes and colors.

COOOOL!

HOW DO FISH BREATHE IN THE WATER? —JOSH, 6, BRITISH COLUMBIA

TO BETTER ANSWER THIS QUESTION, JOSH, WE TOOK A TRIP to the New England Aquarium, in Boston, Massachusetts. At the center of the aquarium is a huge glass tank that rises all the way up through the middle of the floor to the top of the building. Visitors wind their way up a ramp that encircles it and watch the sharks, sea turtles, rays, eels, and fish swimming around. More than a thousand fish live in this large tank! If you were to visit the aquarium, you might notice how the turtles rise to the top of the tank to breathe every now and then . . . but not the fish. Why? Because they don't have to! So, how do fish breathe underwater?

To help us understand how, we spoke with Jo Blasi, an aquarium educator. Like humans, fish need oxygen to survive, but Blasi said they don't breathe with lungs: "They have something called gills, and those gills help them absorb the oxygen from the water, and that oxygen can then go into their blood. And then that blood can go throughout their body, and that oxygen gets to all the places that need it."

GILLS!

Fish's gills are located on the sides of their heads. When fish open their mouths, water runs over their paper-thin gills and pulls oxygen out of the water and into small veins, called capillaries. The blood then takes oxygen to other parts of their bodies, the same way our veins carry oxygenated blood around our bodies.

It's not only fish that have gills. Mollusks (like clams, snails, and scallops) and crustaceans (like shrimp, crabs, and lobsters) also have gills.

Fish have to keep water moving over their gills at all times. "Some fish will swim when they're sleeping. A lot of times those types of fish need water to move over their gills or in their mouth and over their gills to breathe," said Blasi. Some fish will move very slowly while sleeping so they can breathe. But not all fish have to be constantly in motion. Some have a special organ that pumps water over their gills while they sleep or stop moving.

Interestingly, one fish has figured out how to breathe through gills while on land: the mudskipper! Mudskippers live in brackish water. **Brackish** water is a little bit salty but not as salty as the ocean—it usually occurs where rivers meet the sea. Mudskippers can actually jump out of the water and flap their way onto land for short periods of time, where they can breathe as long as they keep their gills moist!

WHY DO PUFFERFISH PUFF UP?

—EERO, 4, WASHINGTON

TO SURVIVE IN AN OCEAN FULL OF PREDATORS, FISH HAVE found various ways to defend themselves. Pufferfish have come up with two unique defenses, and one looks kind of silly!

When threatened by a predator, pufferfish can inflate their bodies, growing up to three times their normal size! This means the bird, seal, or fish trying to eat the pufferfish might not be able to fit its mouth around the pufferfish and might just give up to go search for an easier meal. Or maybe the predators are intimidated by what they thought was a tiny fish suddenly ballooning up into a big one!

Pufferfish may look like balloons, but they're not actually blowing themselves full of air. Because they live in the sea, they're actually gulping large amounts of water to fill their stomachs. They have unique adaptations that make this possible. Firstly, scientists think pufferfish don't use their stomachs to digest food—digestion happens in their intestines. When they're not puffed out, their stomachs are full of folds that expand when they swallow water. They have special muscles in their mouths that work like pumps to pull in water fast, and they can seal off their throats to hold it in. When they are ready to deflate, other muscles help them release the water quickly so they can go about their business.

HOW DO PREDATORS EAT PUFFERFISH IF THEY ARE POISONOUS?—JACK, 4, COLORADO

WHILE IT'S CLEAR THAT PUFFING THEMSELVES UP IS A WAY to protect themselves against predators, this action might actually protect the predators, too! The second defense of pufferfish is poison. Pufferfish have enough poison in their gallbladders to kill thirty adult humans. So predators are usually better off if they don't try to bite into a pufferfish at all.

With those defenses, pufferfish don't have a lot of successful predators. Tiger sharks can eat them, but tiger sharks eat practically anything, including garbage. Sea snakes also eat pufferfish. And there's one other pufferfish predator: humans! These fish are a delicacy in some countries and can only be served by trained chefs who know how to cut out the fish's poison sacs. It's still dangerous, though; a few people die every year trying to eat pufferfish at home. Don't be one of them!

WHAT ARE SEAHORSES?

Seahorses are not horses . . . they're fish! More specifically, they're related to the pipefish. Most pipefish are long, skinny fish with bony armor. Seahorses are named for their horselike snout. They also have curved tails that they use to wrap around seaweed and hold on, which is helpful because they are not very good swimmers.

Seahorses spend most of their time hiding and can change colors using chromatophores (say: crow-MAT-uh-fours), which are color-changing cells in their skin, to camouflage themselves (more on these cells in Chapter 6).

You might have heard that male seahorses give birth to live young. That's not exactly true. Female seahorses deposit eggs into a pouch in a male's body. The males then fertilize the eggs and carry them in the pouch for two weeks or so until they hatch. Seahorses form pairs that live together. They greet each other each morning with a unique dance that can sometimes involve changing colors. Wouldn't that be a fun way to greet your family?

YEE-HAW!

HOW DO JELLYFISH SURVIVE WITHOUT A HEART, LUNGS, OR A BRAIN?—ARAMANI, 8, ALASKA

HERE'S SOMETHING FUNNY! WE JUST LEARNED THAT seahorses are fish . . . not horses. Well, what do you think jellyfish are? Turns out, they're not made out of jelly . . . and they're not fish! However, jellyfish and jelly are both mostly liquid, with just a few solid parts. In fact, jellyfish are 95 percent water!

Jellyfish look kind of like floating balloons with long streamers flowing out behind them. The body of the jellyfish is actually composed of three layers.

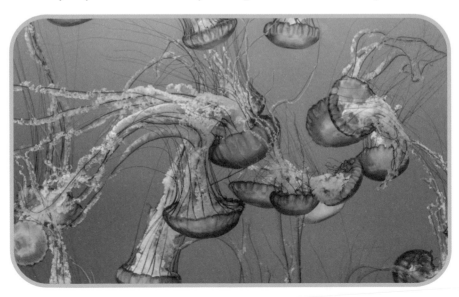

The outer layer is called the epidermis (say: eh-pih-DER-miss). That's the same name as the outer layer on humans, better known as skin. The middle layer is thick, elastic, jelly-like tissue called the **mesoglea** (say: mez-uh-GLEE-uh). The innermost layer is called the **gastrodermis** (say: gas-troh-DER-miss), and that's where digestion happens in a jellyfish. Hanging from the main part of their body, called the **bell**, are the tentacles.

Without brains or hearts, jellyfish are pretty much just stomachs that move around and take in food. "They just move on instinct," Jo Blasi, with the New England Aquarium, told us. "They don't need brains because they don't really have to think about where they're going or what to do to find food."

In place of a brain, jellyfish have two netlike nerve centers. The large nerve net helps the jellyfish sense up and down and dark and light. The smaller nerve net helps them eat and do everything else a jellyfish does. If a jellyfish loses a tentacle or part of its bell, it can continue to function.

Jellyfish don't have a heart because they don't have blood that needs to circulate. All the nutrients and oxygen they need comes directly from the water they live in. Remember, they're mostly water themselves!

HOW DO JELLYFISH SEE?

—CECI, 4, NEW MEXICO

THEY DON'T, CECI! JELLYFISH DON'T HAVE EYES AND THEY don't need to, because, as Blasi told us, "Their food, a lot of time, sort of runs into them; or they carry little plankton that can make food for them." Jellyfish eat the smaller plankton floating around in the ocean. Jellyfish actually *are* a type of zooplankton themselves!

Sometimes they have **oral arms**, tentacles that kind of push food into their stomachs. They can also stun their prey by stinging it with their other tentacles. Those stinging tentacles also help keep any predators away.

Jellyfish look beautiful as they float around in the ocean, but you should keep your distance if you encounter one. Many of them have venom in their tentacles, and it can be painful or dangerous to get stung.

CAREFUL!

CHAPTER 6
OCTOPUSES AND THE CURIOUS CASE OF REGENERATING LIMBS

WITH EIGHT ARMS, COLOR-CHANGING SKIN, AND INK-
squirting abilities, octopuses are some of the coolest
animals in the ocean. So, you might find
it hard to believe that they're related to
something as simple as a clam. Even
though they don't have shells, octopuses
are mollusks just like clams and snails.
Octopuses are **cephalopods** (say: SEF-uh-low-
pods), a group of mollusks that includes squid,
cuttlefish, and nautiluses. What's a cuttlefish,
you ask? Keep reading!

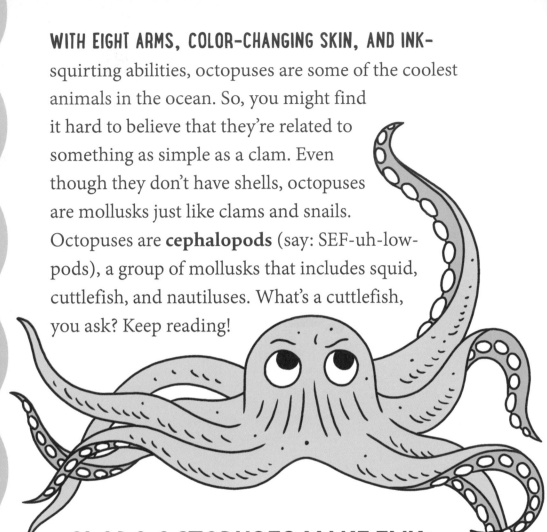

HOW DO OCTOPUSES MAKE INK?
—ISAAC, 4, BRITISH COLUMBIA

CAROLINE ALBERTIN GREW UP FINDING CREATURES IN TIDE
pools and knew she wanted to study ocean life, but her
fascination with octopuses began in graduate school.

"My future adviser took me on a tour of the lab, and in the octopus facility they had a big 250-gallon tank with one little octopus egg in it. And as we were watching, it started moving around in its little clear eggshell—and all of a sudden it hatched out, looked at us, inked, and swam away." From that moment on, Albertin wanted to know more about these ocean predators, and now she's a scientist at the Marine Biological Laboratory, in Woods Hole, Massachusetts.

Octopuses shoot out ink to distract predators and to warn away other cephalopods. Imagine throwing dark liquid in the face of someone who's gotten a little too close to you or tried to eat your dinner! It would certainly make the person stop in their tracks, wouldn't it?

Octopuses aren't the only sea creatures that squirt ink. Some other cephalopods also get to use this cool defense mechanism, too.

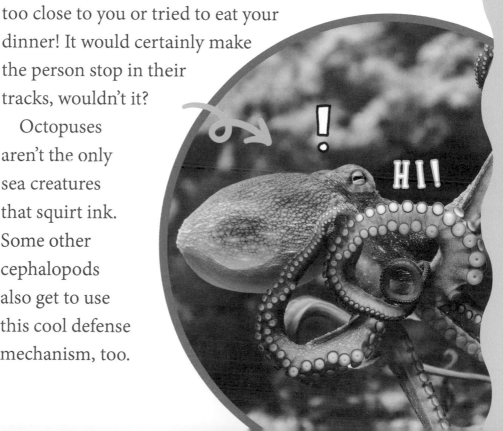

! HI!

They produce ink by combining the contents of two glands. One gland produces **mucus** (basically, snot) and the other gland produces a pigment called **melanin**. Humans have melanin, too; it's what gives our skin and hair their color. The octopus combines the mucus and the melanin together to make ink. So octopus ink is kind of like black snot. *Gross!*

"They can squirt it out with a bunch of mucus stuff and it'll hang in the water, or they can squirt it out without mucus stuff and it just goes everywhere," Albertin said. That ink can block the gills of fish and make them choke. It can even choke octopuses themselves if they can't escape their own ink. In research labs, humans have to clean tanks immediately if the octopus lets out a cloud of ink. "You just don't want to surprise an octopus because it'll just ink and then you have to clean the tank," Albertin added.

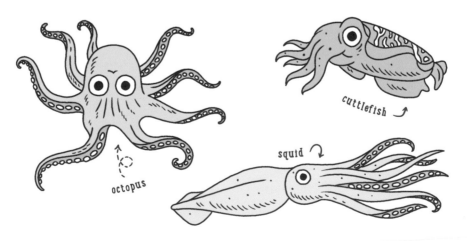

cuttlefish

squid

octopus

SO, WHAT'S A
CUTTLEFISH, THEN?

Like octopuses, cuttlefish are in the cephalopod family. Cuttlefish produce a harmless ink that is used as a food coloring and flavoring in human food. Cuttlefish have a blob-like head and tentacles, and a longer back part of their body, called a mantle, with fins that make it look kind of like it's ruffling when the cuttlefish moves along the ocean floor.

Ink isn't the only thing that makes cephalopods interesting! They're also known for their ability to change color and blend in with their surroundings. The cells in their skin are called chromatophores. These chromatophores have a pigment called ommochromes (say: OHM-oh-cromes) in them. The cells are stretchy. Albertin described it this way: "They've got a bunch of muscles around the outside and they can pull those muscles to expand them out and make them look really big, and then contract them to make them small. And that combination of expanding and contracting will change the color of the animal."

OCTOPUSES HAVE A UNIQUE BODY STRUCTURE. THEY HAVE three hearts: two pump blood to the gills and the third heart pumps blood to other parts of their body. By the way, their blood is copper-based and looks blue. (Your blood is iron-based and looks red.)

Octopuses and cuttlefish have big brains and amazing abilities! Some cuttlefish even passed a test that scientists use to measure self-control. They were able to figure out that instead of taking a treat now, they could wait and get a better treat later. That's something not even all humans can master!

According to Albertin, octopuses interact with the world in a way that's hard for humans to understand: "I was lucky enough to be diving and I saw a day octopus just moving along the reef. And it was changing colors as it went. And it was feeling around in the rocks for things with its suckers. Its suckers are chemosensory"—meaning they have a sense organ—"so they can taste. And so it's exploring its world in a very different way from us. So I think that that's just really mind-boggling." Can you imagine being able to taste things with your arms? Whoa.

HOW DO OCTOPUSES GROW BACK THEIR LIMBS?—BENJI, 5, UTAH

NOT ONLY CAN OCTOPUSES REGROW AN ARM THAT GETS ripped off, but—Caroline Albertin told us—some octopuses can actually throw a limb if they choose! That means they can just detach it from their body! Whether they throw it or lose it another way, once an octopus limb is gone, that arm stump begins to develop a nice little covering with cells in it to cover the wound. Those cells will keep growing into a new arm. No one has found a limit to the number of times an octopus can regrow a limb.

How do they do that? Scientists in Italy determined

that octopuses have a certain protein in their bodies that helps their limbs regrow. They found that levels of this protein began to increase in the octopus's body as soon as it loses one of its eight arms. One hundred days later, when the limb has fully regrown, the protein levels return back to normal. Interestingly, humans have this same protein in our bodies, but in much smaller amounts. This is one reason why we can't regrow our arms and legs.

Octopuses aren't the only animals able to grow back a part of their body. Salamanders and lizards can regrow their tails. Sea stars (aka starfish) and sea cucumbers are able to grow back body parts. Octopus limbs won't regrow an entirely new octopus, but the new limb will be as good as their old one, and that's a skill unique to octopuses. Other animals, like some lizards, can regrow limbs or tails, but the new tail will be of lower quality.

By the way, Albertin told us octopus arms are pretty amazing. "Their arms are what are called 'muscular hydrostats.' This is like your tongue, where they have different groups of muscles that work against each other and so they can move in any direction [and] they can bend at any point."

And each arm has nerve control, meaning it can move on its own without going through the central brain. But, according to Albertin, "that means that they have trouble knowing what their arms are doing if they're not watching them." If a limb gets cut off from the rest of their body, it can even keep moving on its own for a little while.

We humans can't regrow our arms or legs, but at least we always know where they are and what they're doing!

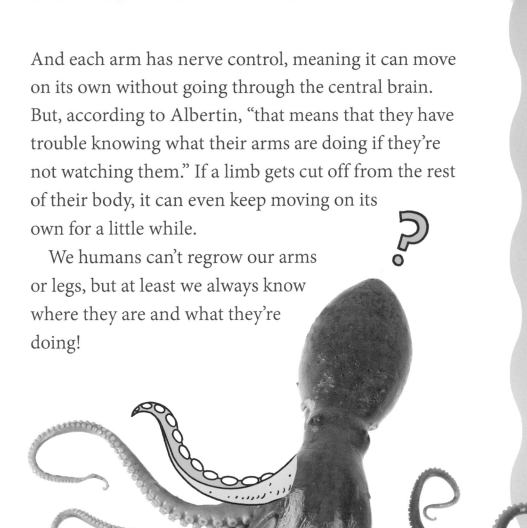

WHAT'S A SQUID?

Squid are close relatives of octopuses. But the two species diverged (separated from one another) more than 270 million years ago in a process called evolution. There are a few important differences:

1. Octopuses stay close to the ocean floor, while squid are more likely to be out in the wide-open ocean.

2. Squid have a triangle-shaped head; octopuses have a more rounded head.

beak

3. Octopuses have eight legs; squid have eight legs and two long feeding tentacles.
Squid can use these extra tentacles to snatch prey out of the ocean from a great distance!

4. And squid have a special kind of protein in their beaks (in the center of their tentacles) that increases its strength.

Scientists aren't entirely sure how many squid species there are, partly because there's such a range in size, and squid grow very rapidly. Most squid species live for only about five years, and in that time the biggest species, the giant squid, will grow to be forty-three feet long!

Giant squid have been the subject of mythology and wild tales for hundreds of years. They have inspired sea monster stories. Some historians believe that sailors who thought they saw sea monsters might actually have been looking at giant squid. Surprisingly, even once scientists knew of the existence of giant squid (from carcasses that washed up on shore), no one was able to capture a picture of a live giant squid in the wild until 2004! These giant cephalopods are as elusive as they are intriguing.

CHAPTER 7
SINGING WHALES, DANCING DOLPHINS, AND THE ENIGMATIC NARWHAL

WHY ARE WHALES SO BIG?

—HUCKLEBERRY, 4, WASHINGTON

YOU MIGHT BE SURPRISED TO KNOW, HUCKLEBERRY, THAT some whales are pretty small! Well, relatively small, anyway. The dwarf sperm whale is the smallest known whale—but it's still taller (or longer, depending how you look at it) than a human. But you're right, some whales are downright gigantic. The blue whale is not only the largest animal on earth today; it's the largest animal that has ever lived! One blue whale was measured at 111 feet (33 meters). That's the length of three yellow school buses! Most blue whales aren't quite that big, averaging between 80 and 100 feet.

Blue whales are a kind
of baleen whale.
Baleen is like a big,
brushy plate inside
the whale's mouth
that catches food
when whales push
water through it. We'll
explain how in just a
minute. Toothed whales
tend to be on the smaller side.

NOM
NOM
NOM

Interestingly, whales haven't always been this big.
To learn more about this, we spoke to Nick Pyenson,
a paleontologist who wrote a book all about whales
and their prehistoric ancestors. **Paleontologists** study
fossils to find out what life was like a long, long time
ago. "For most of the time that whales have been
around on this planet," Pyenson told us, "we don't
find big whales like the ones we see today—like blue
whales, fin whales, right whales, sperm whales. We
don't find those in the fossil record, and we think it
happened very rapidly, very recently."

Now *very recently* doesn't mean the same thing
to a paleontologist as it does to most people. When
Pyenson says recently, he means within the last few

million years! He's looking at the length of time whales have been around—about 50 million years—and saying that, for most of the span of evolutionary time, whales were much smaller. They only started to get really big about four and a half million years ago— pretty recent when you think about it that way.

The **Ice Age** changed the earth's ocean, resulting in a big increase in the type of food that today's big whales prefer to eat: huge schools of krill and small fish. (More on the Ice Age on page 91.) But these

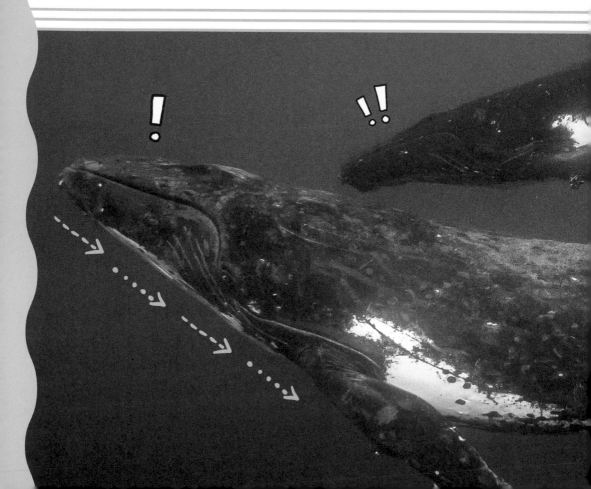

food sources are only in certain parts of the oceans at certain times of year. So, whales began traveling long distances to chase down food sources in their seasonal habitats. Being really big helped these whales travel farther, faster. Their big size also helped make sure they had enough fat or blubber stored in their bodies to give them the energy to get to those food sources during their long migration. Over time, some whales got really, really big—becoming the giants we know and love today.

SO LONG!

YUM!

Baleen whales are very efficient filter feeders. They open their enormous mouths wide and take a big mouthful of water, gulping up all the fish or krill swimming around. Then they close their mouths and push the water out through their baleen, catching all the krill and shrimp in the brush-like filter. It's kind of like straining a pot of pasta through a colander: Water goes down the drain, and the food you want to eat gets left behind.

It's also easier to be huge if you don't have to support your own weight on your legs and feet. Because their bodies are supported as they float around in the water, whales are less limited in their size than they would be on land. Large animals on earth need big bones, and they also need big hearts to pump all that blood around. Since ocean animals can get *so* much bigger than land animals, scientists think there must be other factors at play as well. Maybe someday you'll be the one to help us understand all the reasons whales are so big!

WHAT WAS THE ICE AGE?

Imagine if winter never ended. Scientists think that's what happens during something called an ice age. Over the course of the earth's history, the climate and landscape has changed dramatically, and at various times most of the earth's land has been covered by ice. There have been at least five major ice ages in the earth's history. The most recent ice age began 120,000 years ago and ended about 15,000 years ago. That sounds like a long time ago. And it is, in human years. But in the overall age of the earth, remember, that was pretty recently!

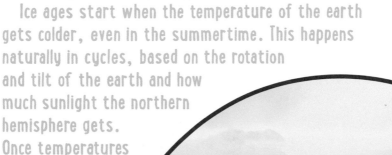

Ice ages start when the temperature of the earth gets colder, even in the summertime. This happens naturally in cycles, based on the rotation and tilt of the earth and how much sunlight the northern hemisphere gets. Once temperatures get cold enough that the snow doesn't melt in summertime, the buildup of snow can help make the atmosphere get colder and colder.

Here's how Ross MacPhee, curator at the American Museum of Natural History, explained this theory of never-ending winter: "You'd have snowfalls in the winter and it never really got warm enough to get rid of it completely. The next year that [snow] would be built on, and built on, and built on. And the thing about snow, as those who live in snowy regions know, is that it kind of makes its own local weather." Meaning, just having snow on the ground makes the air colder.

"If you have enough snow, then it's very cold," MacPhee continued. "That tends to preserve the snowpack for a very long period of time." (Think hundreds of years.) "If that process continues over a very long period of time, then what you're going to get is not just snow, but the snow is going to be compacted because it's water, it weighs something. And as it compacts, it turns to ice. And that gives us the ice at the Ice Age."

Think of your favorite sledding hill. If you keep going down the hill on your sled and then walking back up, that sledding trail gets packed down, turning from light fluffy snow to something that feels more like ice. It's kind of the same thing, but on a much, much bigger scale, when it comes to the Ice Age.

If you looked at a world map during the Ice Age, the northern United States and all of Canada, as well as northern Europe and parts of northern Asia, would be all covered with big sheets of ice. You'd also notice something else: North America was connected to Russia by a land bridge! That's because so much of the earth's water was frozen in the ice sheets that the ocean level was three hundred feet lower than it is today. So humans and other animals could use that uncovered land to travel from one continent to the other. Animals and humans used that land bridge to travel between the two continents.

The Ice Age ended sometime around fifteen thousand years ago with another shift in the climate to warmer temperatures. As the Ice Age ended, a number of large species of animals, like mammoths, saber-toothed tigers, and giant land sloths died out. Also as the ice melted, the level of the ocean rose to where it is today.

Why are we telling you all of this in a book about the ocean? Well, the Ice Age had a big impact on the world's ocean and everything that lives in it as well!

TIMELINE

MANY OF THE ANIMALS AND PLANTS THAT LIVE IN THE OCEAN existed on earth way before *Homo sapiens* (that's us humans!). Earth is estimated to be 460 billion years old, and most of the species in the ocean have been around for millions of years.

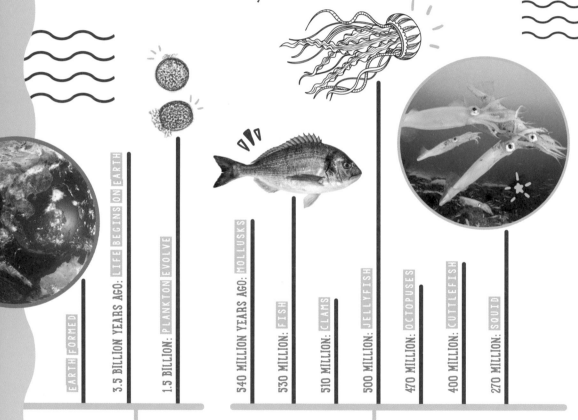

EARTH FORMED

3.5 BILLION YEARS AGO: LIFE BEGINS ON EARTH

1.5 BILLION: PLANKTON EVOLVE

540 MILLION YEARS AGO: MOLLUSKS

530 MILLION: FISH

510 MILLION: CLAMS

500 MILLION: JELLYFISH

470 MILLION: OCTOPUSES

400 MILLION: CUTTLEFISH

270 MILLION: SQUID

PRECAMBRIAN ERA
4.6 BILLION–
541 MILLION
YEARS AGO

PALEOZOIC ERA
541 MILLION–
251 MILLION
YEARS AGO

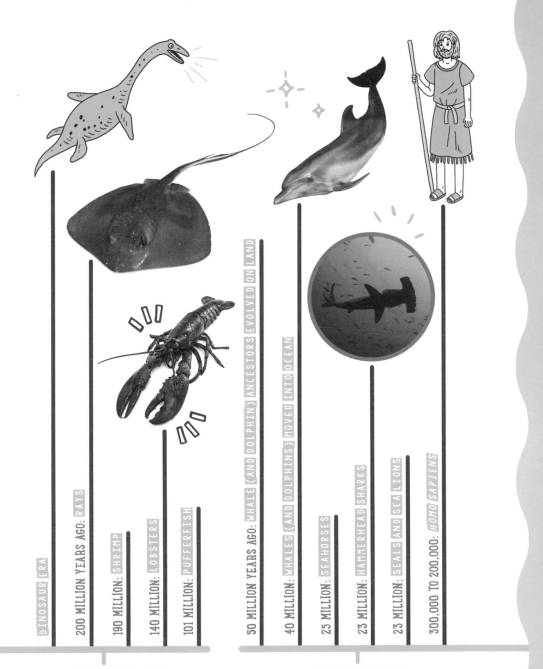

DINOSAUR ERA

200 MILLION YEARS AGO: RAYS

190 MILLION: SHRIMP

140 MILLION: LOBSTERS

101 MILLION: PUFFERFISH

WHALE (AND DOLPHIN) ANCESTORS EVOLVED ON LAND

WHALES (AND DOLPHINS) MOVED INTO OCEAN

50 MILLION YEARS AGO:

40 MILLION:

25 MILLION: SEAHORSES

23 MILLION: HAMMERHEAD SHARKS

23 MILLION: SEALS AND SEA LIONS

300,000 TO 200,000: *HOMO SAPIENS*

MESOZOIC ERA
251 MILLION–
66 MILLION
YEARS AGO

CENOZOIC ERA
66 MILLION YEARS AGO–NOW
|
ICE AGE: 120,000–15,000 YEARS AGO

HOW DO WHALES SING?

—DOMINIC, 8, NORTH CAROLINA

TO FIND OUT THIS ANSWER, WE SPOKE WITH AMY VAN CISE, a biologist with NOAA's Northwest Fisheries Science Center, in Seattle, Washington. Van Cise has spent a lot of time studying whale communication and told us, "The way that whales produce sounds is really similar to the way humans produce sounds."

Van Cise said, "In humans, we have what's called a **larynx** (say: LAYR-inx) in our throats, and that larynx has a bunch of vocal folds. We push air through those vocal folds and it makes them vibrate and flap around. And those vibrations are what produces sound."

Of course, when humans make sounds, our voices are normally traveling through the air. But for whales, that sound is traveling through water, which not only makes it sound different, but can affect how far away it can be heard.

"Song is actually mostly a mating behavior, so it's only the males that sing," Van Cise told us. Baleen whales like humpbacks are the only whales known to sing. (Other whales make a series of different kinds of sounds, like clicks and chatters, but don't make sounds that we would characterize as a song. Van Cise specializes in pilot whales, one of the species that click and chatter instead of singing.)

Researchers still have a lot to learn about why some whales sing. They're working to understand the very complicated songs of the humpback whale in particular, and why individuals of that species slowly change their songs over the course of many years.

While whales use their songs to communicate, humans sometimes use whale sounds to relax! People have even added whale songs to music. In fact, a whole album called *Songs of the Humpback Whale* consists only of whale songs! The album sold more than one hundred thousand copies when it first came out more than fifty years ago, and is credited with helping start the "Save the Whales" movement in the 1970s, which lead to greater conservation for these threatened animals.

WHY DO NARWHALS HAVE HORNS?
—MIKA, 6, NEW JERSEY

NARWHALS ARE NOT WATER UNICORNS, THOUGH THEY KIND of look like they could be! Narwhals are a species of toothed whales, and that "horn" is a tusk—just like you'd find on a walrus or elephant. A **tusk** is just an oversized tooth that can't fit in a mouth. And despite what it looks like, their "horn" doesn't grow out of their forehead; it's actually coming out of their lip. Narwhals can grow up to seventeen feet long, and that tooth can be an additional nine feet!

So, what is this tooth for? Scientists don't know much about narwhals, so they only have some theories—and there's still a lot more to learn. Narwhals live in frigid water above the Arctic Circle, and for about half of the year they live under an ice sheet. Some scientists speculate that they use their tusk to break the ice to breathe. Another theory is that narwhals may use their tusks for fighting.

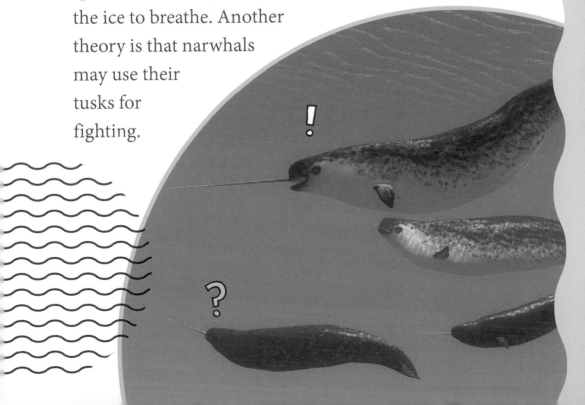

In 2017, though, Canadian researchers observing narwhals by drone finally got some video evidence that suggests these sneaky whales use their tusks for hunting. No, they weren't spearing fish with their tusks. Instead, they whacked fish with them, stunning their prey before gulping them down!

WHY DO DOLPHINS JUMP OUT OF THE WATER?—TYSON, 6, CALIFORNIA

IT'S AN AMAZING SIGHT TO SEE DOLPHINS LEAPING OUT OF the water like aquatic acrobats! Spinner dolphins add a spin to their leap—showoffs! It's not just dolphins; other members of the **cetacean** (say: sih-TAY-shun) group (whales, dolphins, and porpoises are cetaceans) can leap into the air, too, including the forty-ton humpback whale. Now that makes a splash!

Scientists think there are a number of reasons dolphins like to jump. They can hold their breath for up to twelve minutes, but since they don't have gills, dolphins have to come to the surface to breathe air. So, when they leap out of the water, they can take a breath at the same time.

Another reason could be that when dolphins take a leap, they use it as an opportunity to look around. Maybe they're checking out the coastline or looking for other members of their pod.

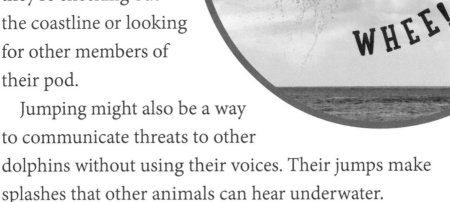

WHEE!

Jumping might also be a way to communicate threats to other dolphins without using their voices. Their jumps make splashes that other animals can hear underwater.

But there are other ideas, too. They may jump to show leadership. And one particularly surprising theory is that jumping cleans parasites off their skin, as the impact of hitting the water may scrape the parasites off. And it might feel good, kind of like scratching an itch. Or they might just jump for the sheer fun of it!

So, how do they get their bodies out of the water? Dolphins are fast and efficient swimmers. Normally, they cruise around at three to seven miles per hour. When they want to jump out of the water, they increase their speed to around twenty-five miles an hour, which allows them to break the surface and leap into the air.

CHAPTER 8
A (BRIEF) HISTORY OF THE OCEAN AND GLOBAL TRADING

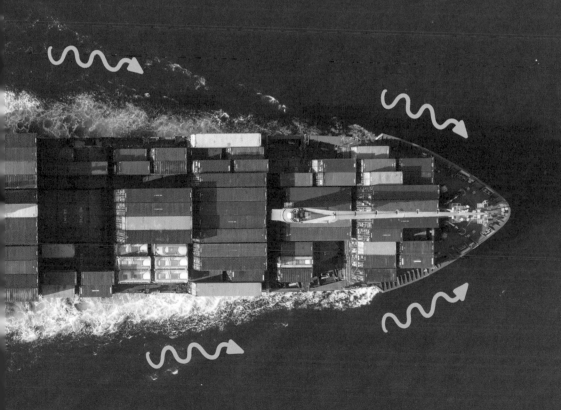

HAVE YOU EVER WONDERED WHY MOST OF THE WORLD'S

biggest cities are close to the ocean? If you take a look at a map, you'll notice that cities like Mumbai, New York, São Paulo, Shanghai, and Tokyo all have access to the ocean. There's a good chance that you live near the ocean, too! NOAA estimates that 40 percent of Americans live in a county with a coastline. Why is that?

Humans have lived near the ocean for thousands of years. After the last ice age, humans transitioned away from being hunter gatherers to planting crops and domesticating animals. For a long time, we thought humans started using boats around the end of the last ice age, but new evidence points to humans using boats much earlier. Boats were used to expand the human population around the world. Early humans may have crossed the land bridge into North America from Asia during the Ice Age, or they may have traveled down the coast by small boats.

When people started to become farmers, they found the best land for planting crops was near rivers, because the seasonal flooding brought more nutrients to the land. Eventually those settlements moved to the coastlines because humans found the weather to be more moderate (less harsh) and there was plenty to eat! Scientists have found that these early people were eating fish, shellfish, ocean mammals, and ocean plants, too. Eventually, big cities were established by the sea. Not only was there abundant food, but as trading became more established, living near the ocean was convenient for being able to come and go.

OCEAN EXPLORERS

Humans have been sailing across the ocean for centuries, exploring new parts of the world and conducting trade between different regions. Vikings explored North America a thousand years ago and created early trade routes by land and ocean between Africa and the Middle East (Persia). In the fifteenth century, European explorers came to North America. As boats became bigger and humans learned more about navigation, the ocean was what allowed people to trade goods and culture.

Trade between cultures wasn't always peaceful. Many wars were fought over control of the ocean. Pirates were a threat to ships, and life on the ocean was dangerous.

People have long looked for different routes for trade around the world, and while searching for new routes, they explored different parts of the world. Trading also led to engineering. The Panama Canal and the Suez Canal were built to connect waterways so ships could pass through. Canals are sort of man-made rivers.

THE OCEAN ECONOMY NOW

Even today, huge ocean liners cross the globe carrying food, cars, furniture, toys, and more. Ninety percent of the goods traded between countries travels across the ocean. The importance of global shipping became very clear in 2021, when a boat was stuck in the Suez Canal and slowed down shipping around the world for weeks.

The laws of the ocean have been established through international treaties (agreements), so that everyone knows the rules, no matter what country the ships are coming from. But, conflicts do come up between countries for control of marine resources, and there are still pirates in some parts of the ocean.

The ocean is still an important part of the global food system. In 2017, fish protein accounted for 17 percent of the world's animal protein intake, according to the United Nations. And it's not just fishing that's feeding the world. As demand for seafood keeps increasing, countries are investing in aquaculture—fish farming. In the United States we grow oysters, clams, mussels, shrimp, seaweed, and some fish species.

Seaweed is another important ocean food source. You might be a familiar with nori, which is used to wrap sushi rolls. Dried seaweed is a popular snack food in many countries. Seaweed is also used in a lot of foods you might not expect, often in the form of an ingredient called **carrageenan** (say: care-uh-JEE-nin): It is sometimes used to thicken ice cream and pudding. It's probably even in your toothpaste. Beyond its use in food, seaweed is often an ingredient in makeup and animal feed and used as a fertilizer on farms.

There's yet another important way the ocean contributes to the world: tourism. People who don't live near the ocean love to take trips to the seaside. Many ocean cities are there because people like to have fun! NOAA says there are 3.3 million jobs in the United States that are related to the ocean, and three quarters of those jobs are in tourism.

CHAPTER 9
SHARKS!

WHY DO SHARKS HAVE SHARP TEETH?—AIDEN, 6, NEW HAMPSHIRE

IF THERE'S ONE THING PEOPLE TEND TO THINK ABOUT WHEN they hear the word *shark*, Aiden, it's probably a row (or many rows) of very sharp teeth!

Sharks have sharp teeth for the same reason other carnivores and predators have sharp teeth—they need them to bite their prey. Almost all sharks are **carnivores** (meaning their diet primarily consists of meat), so they don't need flat grinding teeth like **omnivores** (animals that eat plants and meat) or **herbivores** (plant-eating animals). Some sharks are bottom-feeders and are part of the ocean cleanup crew. Larger sharks—like the great white shark—will eat big fish like salmon and stingrays, and also seals. Researchers are extremely careful when studying or handling sharks and their sharp teeth. When we spoke with Kady Lyons of the

Georgia Aquarium, she had just returned from a shark expedition—for research, of course! Sharks are a very diverse group of fish. Lyons says those differences are apparent in all the types of teeth they can have. While humans and other primates have teeth that look similar from one species to another, sharks have all kinds of different-looking mouths!

"You have everything from your big megalodon great white shark tooth all the way down to some that just have like plates. So they're sucking in their prey and they're crushing their prey." (**Megalodons** were enormous prehistoric sharks that no longer exist.)

Here's a neat example: The frilled shark has needlelike teeth that point inward to move food into their mouths. What makes them so unusual is that their teeth are arranged in evenly spaced rows with gaps in between. It's a very neat and pretty arrangement, but good luck seeing them in the wild— these sharks are very rare.

The cookie-cutter shark has rows of teeth that are fused together. So, when it loses a tooth it doesn't lose a single one—it loses a whole row! These rare, tiny sharks also are known for eating the teeth they lose to retain their nutrients. But we wouldn't recommend trying to eat your own teeth.

HAVE YOU EVER FOUND A SHARK TOOTH ON THE BEACH?

Shark teeth wash up frequently on beaches because sharks have a lot of teeth to lose. Each shark can produce thirty thousand to fifty thousand teeth in their lifetime! Some sharks lose a tooth a week. Their teeth aren't attached to the gums with roots the way our human

teeth are. It only takes a day for a shark to grow a new tooth when one falls out. In many species the teeth are arranged in rows. So, when one tooth falls out, the tooth behind it moves forward. Most sharks have five to fifteen rows of teeth. The great white has up to seven rows.

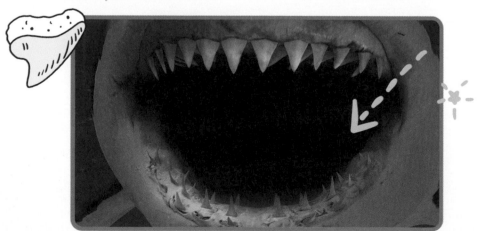

ALSO WORTH NOTING IS THAT MOST SHARKS DON'T REALLY chew. Instead, they use their teeth to grab prey and sometimes rip it into more bite-size pieces that they can then swallow. But a few species—like whale sharks, basking sharks, and megamouth sharks—are filter feeders, eating plankton and krill, just like baleen whales. They don't have baleen, though. Instead, they have comb-like filters at the backs of their throats that let water through while holding on to their tiny prey.

Sharks don't always choose their prey very carefully. Scientists have found plastic, metal, even a chicken coop in sharks' stomachs. "I think the tiger shark is definitely known as the garbage dump of the shark. They get the dumpster-diving credit among sharks and rays," Lyons said.

On those rare occasions when people are attacked by sharks, the humans are often on surfboards or using flippers, which might confuse a shark into thinking the person is a seal or other animal it considers prey!

WHY DO HAMMERHEAD SHARKS HAVE A HAMMERHEAD?

—HUDSON, 4, BRITISH COLUMBIA

THEY DO CERTAINLY HAVE AN UNUSUAL HEAD SHAPE, DON'T they, Hudson?

Hammerhead sharks have a flat, wide head that juts out from either side of its body, with eyes very far apart at either end. That's by design; their wide-set eyes give them a broad field of vision. And seeing a lot of the ocean gives them an advantage in spotting their prey.

That hammer-like head gives them another advantage—these sharks have been observed using their heads to pin fish to the seafloor before eating them.

While that head shape helps with hunting, it also makes them vulnerable to getting trapped by their heads in large fishing nets.

HOW DO STINGRAYS STING?

—LOUIS, 5, AUSTRALIA

STINGRAYS ARE DELIGHTFUL SEA FLAP-FLAPS THAT ARE WIDE and flat and kind of ripple through the water when they swim. A stingray's mouth even looks like a permanent smile! But don't be fooled by their friendly appearance—these shark cousins have a dangerous way to defend themselves.

Stingrays have a long tail with a **barb** (a spike) at the end that carries a deadly toxin. The barb is serrated, meaning it has a sharp, jagged edge like a steak knife. Stingrays lie flat on the ocean floor, sometimes covered by a thin layer of sand, making them basically invisible to prey (and to beachgoers, who occasionally step on them and get stung!). While the stings are painful, most of the time they're not deadly.

The stingray's flat shape allows it to blend in with the ocean floor. Its mouth is on the underside of its body, so it can eat all the worms, clams, and shrimp it finds down there. Meanwhile, its eyes are on top of its body, so it can see predators and obstacles around it. Interestingly, the shape of a stingray's teeth changes depending on the season! Most of the time, stingrays have round flat teeth, but in mating season, their teeth turn sharp and pointy.

But not all rays sting! Some don't even have stingers at all.

Rays and sharks are very cool animals that play important roles in the ocean ecosystem. There's no need to be afraid of them. Sharks, in particular, get a bad rap for being aggressive killers. But, remember, shark attacks are extremely rare. And when they do attack, sharks aren't being mean—they're just doing what sharks do: hunt prey! So pay attention if there are signs at the beach warning of sharks in the area.

If you love sharks, one of the things you can do to protect them is to learn more about climate change. Kady Lyons of the Georgia Aquarium worries about how climate change will have a direct impact on the sharks she studies: "We have no idea how that's going to throw off the balance of the base of the food chain, and just those ripple effects that go through, including habitat destruction of the nursery grounds that these animals use." As you may have learned in school, living things need a healthy ecosystem (plants and animals and the landscape they live in) to thrive. If climate change affects just one part of an ecosystem, it could throw off the balance for every organism that relies on it. Lyons says scientists are watching what happens with sharks very carefully, because their health could be a clue to how other animals might fare as the ocean changes.

CHAPTER 10
SEA LIONS, WALRUSES, AND SEALS THAT BARK

WHY DO SEALS BARK?

—ROWAN, 6, NORTH CAROLINA

BECAUSE THEY'RE MERMAID DOGS! JUST KIDDING, ROWAN. Seals, sea lions, and walruses are part of an animal family called **pinnipeds** (say: PIN-uh-peds), which means *fin-footed*. These are mammals that spend their time in the ocean and on land. They share common ancestors with bears, which also make vocalizations that sound kind of like barking!

Katie Sweeney, a biologist at the Alaska Fisheries Science Center, thinks we might associate those sounds with barking because humans are familiar with dogs. All these animals can make similar sounds. Sweeney studies a type of sea lion called Steller sea lions, and she says the noise they make is closer to a roar! That roaring noise might be part of the reason we call them sea "lions." The males also have a big ruff of fur that looks like a lion's mane to some people. They use it as padding when they fight with other males.

walrus

seal

sea lion

According to Sweeney, the reason they bark is probably for the same reasons humans talk: "They're communicating to their fellow sea lions. They're trying to locate their pups, maybe. Pup and mother pairs will call to each other and they can recognize each other's calls and then find each other, and then they can recognize each other's smells as well. You'll see a female come up on a beach and her pup could be anywhere and she'll just eventually zero in on the pup and find it, even if the pup moves."

Like humans, seals and sea lions have a larynx

(voice box) and are able to produce sounds by sending air through their vocal cords. Except, unlike land mammals, they can also whistle, chirp, click, and even clap underwater!

While seals and sea lions spend part of their time on land, they are really in their element when they're in the water. They are strong swimmers, and they go into the water to hunt for fish. Even when they're in the water, they need to come to the surface to breathe air (because they're mammals). Most seals can hold their breath for fifteen minutes, but some species can hold their breath for up to eighty! In the Arctic and Antarctic, they often have to break holes in the ice with their heads to find a spot to breathe.

HELLO?

?

WHAT'S A WALRUS?

Sure, they may look like hippos, but walruses are part of the same pinniped group as seals and sea lions.

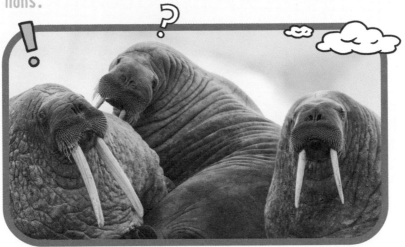

Walruses are ginormous! If you've ever seen one at a zoo or an aquarium, you've probably noticed that they are almost as big as a car. They weigh anywhere from 800 to 3,700 pounds, and have a layer of blubber and thick skin to keep warm. In the wild they have to find sea ice strong enough to support their weight when they want to relax out of the water! Walruses aren't great swimmers and tend to stay in shallow areas to hunt for food.

What makes walruses so striking to look at are their giant tusks. Those two front teeth can be up to three feet long, and walruses use them like ice picks to help lift their big bodies up onto the ice, or to break holes in the ice from under the water when they need to make a breathing hole.

CHAPTER 11
THE OCEAN AND YOU!

NOW THAT YOU KNOW MORE ABOUT THE BIODIVERSITY OF life in the ocean, you know that the health of the ocean is important to the health of the world. But ocean life is threatened by humans through climate change and pollution. So, what can one kid do?

First, let's talk about climate change. Climate change threatens the health of the whole planet, including the plants and animals that live in the ocean. (See page 9 for more on climate change.)

Taking steps to combat climate change in your home and advocating for change at a national level can help.

Here are some steps you (and your household) can take to combat climate change:

1. Conserve water. Turn off water while brushing your teeth. Take a shower instead of a bath.

2. Stop using pesticides on your lawn. Pesticides are chemicals used on plants to try to keep bugs and other pests away, but all of those chemicals can end up in storm drains and eventually the ocean.

3. Make sure your cleaning products are biodegradable. Chemicals in cleaning products can end up in the ocean.

TURN OFF THE WATER!

4. Stop using single-use plastics (think of all that plastic trash

in the great garbage patch). If you live near a beach, make it a habit to pick up trash on the shoreline.

5. It's okay to eat seafood, but make sure you're buying fish and shellfish that have been raised or caught in a way that doesn't harm the overall population. There are websites where you and your adults can learn more about sustainable fishing.

6. If you fish or catch crabs, make sure you're following the rules on catch limits. If your family has a boat, use it responsibly and obey "no-wake" zones.

You can also get involved with ocean conservation organizations, even while you're young. Some of these groups need volunteer help and might have opportunities for families to volunteer. You can also think of ways to raise money to donate to environmental groups, maybe by collecting bottles or having a bake sale or selling crafts.

Encourage the adults in your life to support politicians, leaders, and businesses that care about the environment. You can write letters and emails to elected officials to urge them to support laws that protect the ocean.

WHAT ARE SOME JOBS THAT INVOLVE THE OCEAN?

Do you want to make the ocean part of your life as an adult? If so, there are lots of jobs that will keep you near the ocean. Some even involve scuba diving!

If you love the ocean and science, consider studying to become a **marine biologist** or an **oceanographer** or even a **marine archaeologist**. There are also **engineers** who work in the ocean, and **ocean hydrologists** (people who study water and the way it flows). There are many colleges where you can get 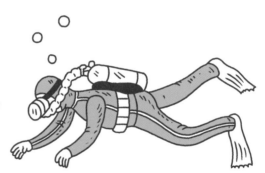 degrees or certificates in these fields, which will help you find a career studying the ocean.

Maybe you're passionate about animal care? If so, you could study **marine biology** or become a **veterinarian**. Some of these people become **marine wildlife rescuers and rehabilitators**.

If you're concerned about the environment, you might consider studying **environmental science** and working for an **ocean conservation** group.

Maybe you're fascinated by big ships and want to spend your days at sea. Consider joining your country's **navy** or becoming a **merchant mariner**. That's someone who works on big boats, shipping products around the world. There are maritime colleges specifically for people who want to work on boats.

Or maybe you'd like to become a fisherman. There's no degree needed for that, but you might want to do some research to figure out what kind of **fisherman** or **fisherwoman** you'd like to be!

Lots of people do other kinds of jobs at sea. Everything from **lifeguarding** to working on a **cruise ship** to becoming a **commercial diver** to being a professional **surfer** or **sailboat racer**!

There are lots of ways to stay close to the ocean as you grow up—whether it's through an ocean-based career or just as someone who enjoys the sea and wants to help protect it. Spread the word—talk to your friends, family, and classmates about the importance of keeping the ocean healthy and diverse.

A NOTE FROM THE AUTHORS

For as long as humans have existed, we have relied on the sea, and wanted to learn more about it. Technological advances have also helped humans explore below the surface of the water. We now know so much about everything from how much salt is in the ocean to what the landscape on the bottom of the ocean looks like, to many of the plants and animals that call the ocean home.

But there's still so much more to discover. Scientists are constantly learning about animal species they've never identified before. Or how the ocean currents impact the climate on land. Or what the land and ocean looked like millions of years ago.

We hope this book has piqued your curiosity, but there's a lot more to learn! Maybe someday *you* will contribute to our understanding of the world ocean!

As we always say: Stay curious!

—Jane & Melody

GLOSSARY

ANADROMOUS (uh-NAD-ruh-muss): Fish that live in salt water but are born in fresh water and return to fresh water to spawn (reproduce). Catadromous (cuh-TAD-ruh-muss) fish do the opposite. They are born in salt water, live their lives in fresh water, and return to salt water to spawn.

ANEMONES (uh-NEM-uh-nees): Brightly colored polyps with clusters of tentacles that resemble flowers

ARTHROPODS (ARTH-roh-pods): Animals without spines, many of which (like insects and crustaceans) have armor-like exoskeletons on the outside

BALEEN (bay-LEEN): Large brushy plates inside the mouths of some whales that allow them to filter feed. There are two groups of whales: baleen whales and toothed whales (whales with teeth instead of baleen).

BAY: A small inlet of the ocean, mostly surrounded by a significant amount of land

CETACEANS (sih-TAY-shuns): Aquatic mammals that resemble fish but breathe air; includes porpoises, dolphins, and whales

CEPHALOPODS (SEF-uh-low-pods): A subsection of mollusks, cephalopods have arms. While most mollusks have shells, several cephalopods don't: cuttlefish, octopuses, and squid. Nautilus are cephalopods with shells.

COVE: A small, sheltered bay

CRUSTACEANS (crust-AY-shins): A group of arthropods that live partially in the water. They are invertebrates (no backbone); most have a hard outer shell (exoskeleton) and legs with many segments. They breathe using gills, like fish.

ECHINODERMS (ee-KYE-nuh-derms): A group of marine animals that live only in salt water and have spiny skin and a body that radiates out from the center. Echinoderms include sea urchins, sea cucumbers, sea stars, and sea lilies.

FOSSIL FUELS: Fuel sources including coal, oil, and natural gas that were formed underground from plants and animals over a long period of time

FRICTION: The resistance between two objects as they try to move past each other

GULF: A section of ocean that extends far inland and has a narrow opening. Examples include the Gulf of Mexico and the Gulf of Alaska

INVERTEBRATES (In-VER-tuh-bretts): Animals without backbones

ISTHMUS (ISTH-mis): A narrow band of land with ocean on both sides

LARYNX (LAYR-inx): The part of the air tube in an animal's throat that contains the vocal cords, which enables us to speak and other mammals to make vocal sounds

MOLLUSKS: A group of invertebrates (creatures without backbones) that usually have a shell. Examples include clams, mussels, snails, slugs, limpets, squid, octopuses, and nautiluses.

OCEAN: The body of salt water that covers most of the earth; it can also mean one of the five named oceans that make up part of this water (Antarctic or Southern Ocean, Arctic Ocean, Atlantic Ocean, Indian Ocean, and Pacific Ocean).

OMMOCHROME (OHM-oh-crome): A kind of pigment (or coloring), usually found in the eyes of insects and crustaceans. It is also found in the skin of some fish to enable them to change color.

PINNIPEDS (PIN-uh-peds): An order of mammals that lives in the water, including seals, sea lions, and walruses

SEA: A named section of an ocean

STRAIT: A narrow waterway between two bigger bodies of water

TIDE: The movement of water pulled by the sun and moon

TRENCH: Very low areas in the ocean floor

TUSK: A large tooth that can't fit in an animal's mouth. They can be found on narwhals and walruses.

MORE *BUT WHY!*

AT *BUT WHY*, WE DO A LOT MORE THAN WRITE ABOUT THE ocean. We put out a new episode of our podcast every two weeks, and *you* can be a part of it! We take questions from kids all around the world—just like you—and we find the answers. You can listen to all our episodes at www.butwhykids.org, and that's where you'll also learn how to ask a question of your own that might get used in one of our episodes. We tackle all kinds of topics— whatever *you* are curious about, from who invented words to why babies take so long to grow up.

BUT WHY IS PRODUCED BY VERMONT PUBLIC RADIO. YOU CAN LEARN MORE ABOUT VPR AT WWW.VPR.ORG.

AND CHECK OUT OUR OTHER BOOK, ARE LLAMAS TICKLISH?